JAZZ FAVORITES

Arranged by Bill Boyd

ISBN 978-0-7935-3309-1

HAL•LEONARD™ CORPORATION

7777 W. BLUEMOUND RD. P.O. BOX 13819 MILWAUKEE, WI 53213

JAZZ FAVORITES

ALICE IN WONDERLAND
(From Walt Disney's "ALICE IN WONDERLAND")

Words by BOB HILLIARD
Music by SAMMY FAIN

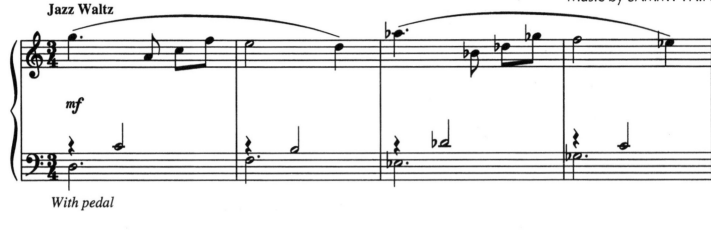

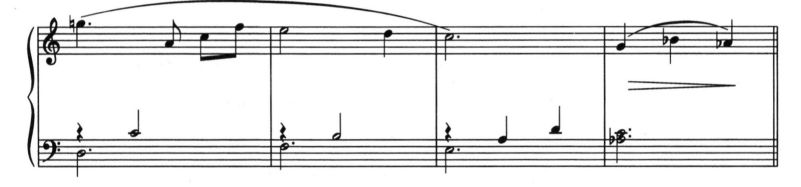

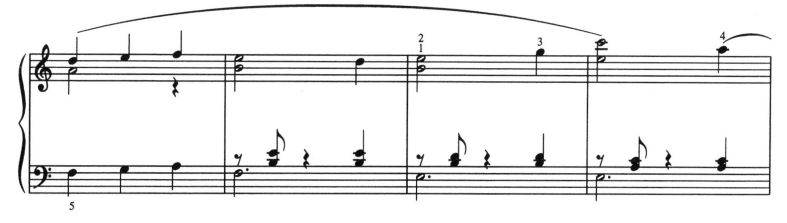

add pedal

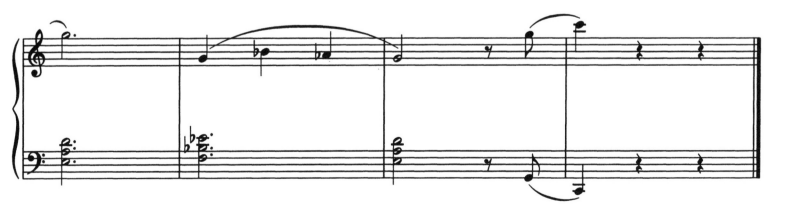

APRIL IN PARIS

Words by E. Y. HARBURG
Music by VERNON DUKE

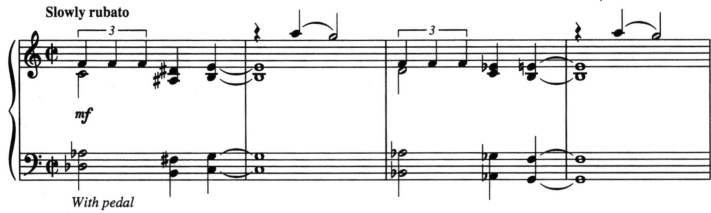

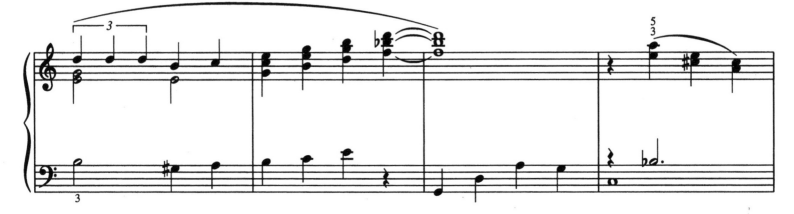

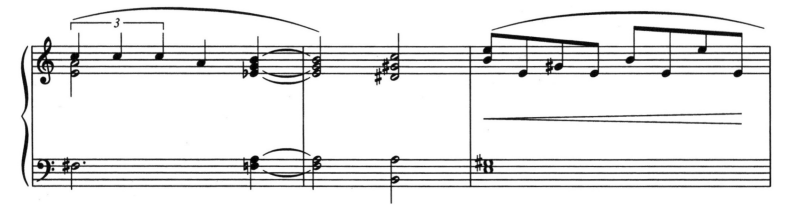

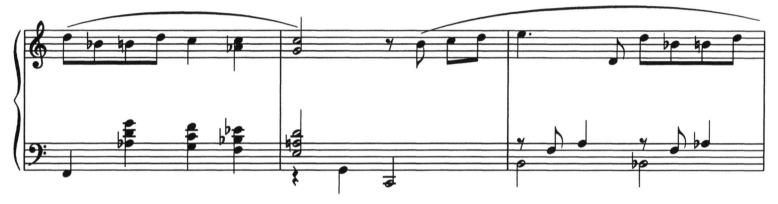

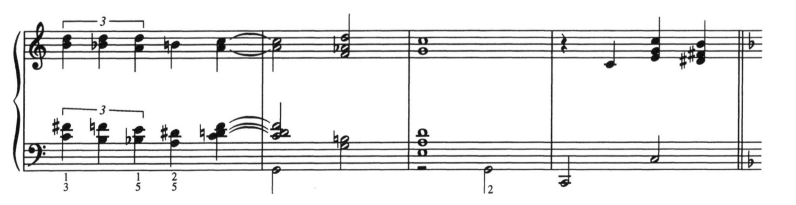

Steady tempo (♪♪ played as ♪³♪)

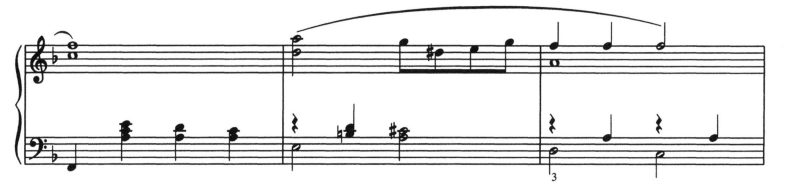

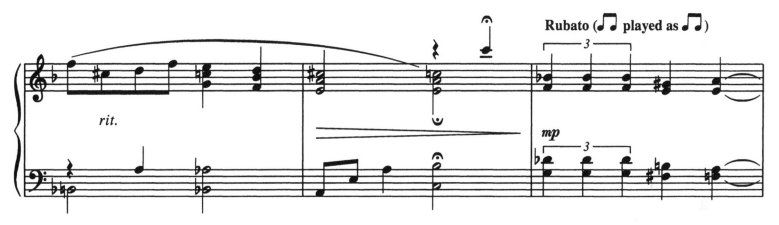

Rubato (♫ played as ♩♪)

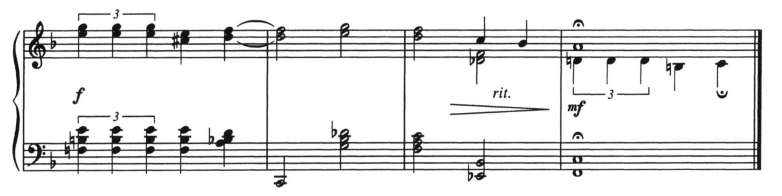

BODY AND SOUL

Words by EDWARD HEYMAN,
ROBERT SOUR and FRANK EYTON
Music by JOHN GREEN

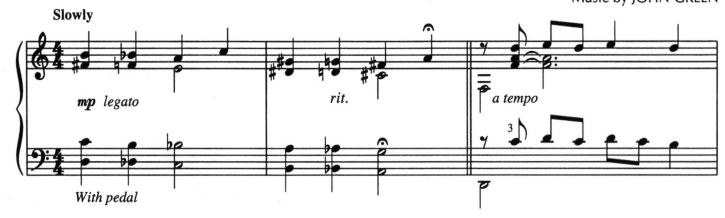

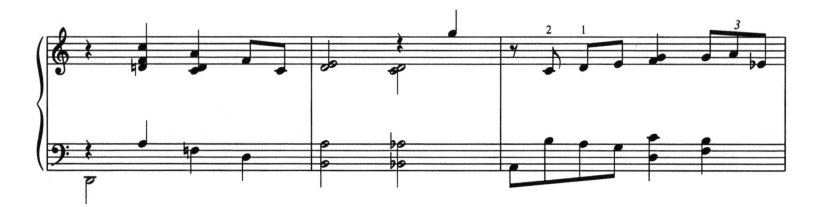

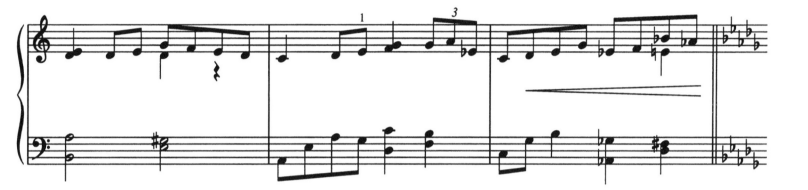

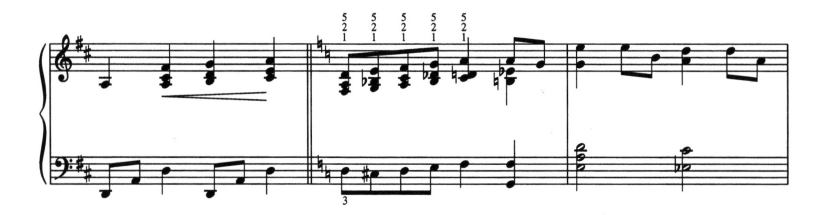

DON'T GET AROUND MUCH ANYMORE

Words and Music by BOB RUSSELL
and DUKE ELLINGTON

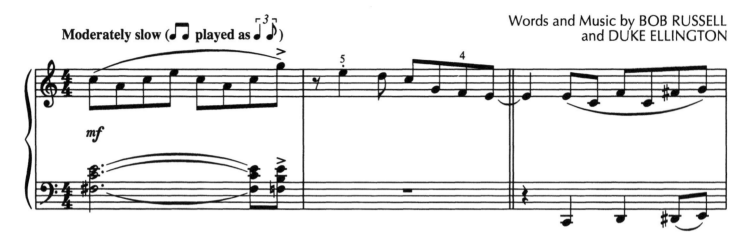

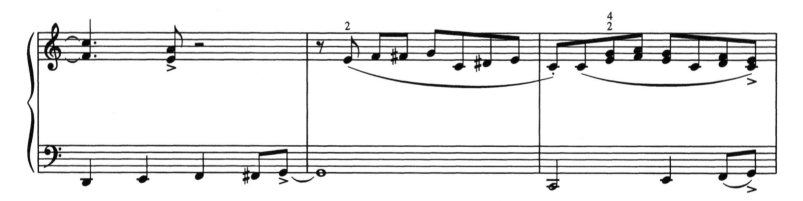

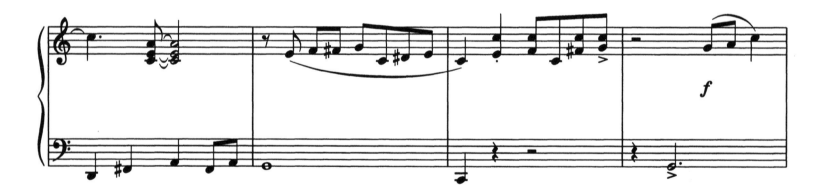

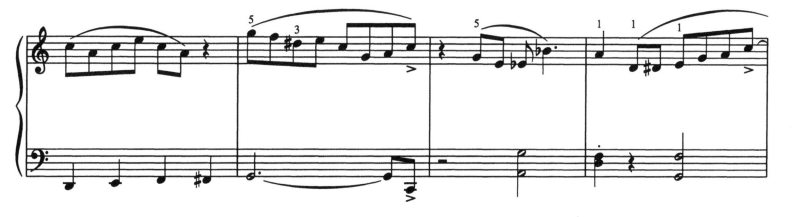

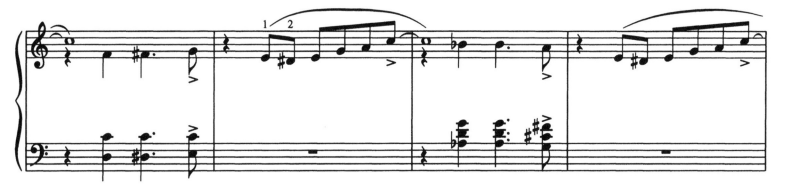

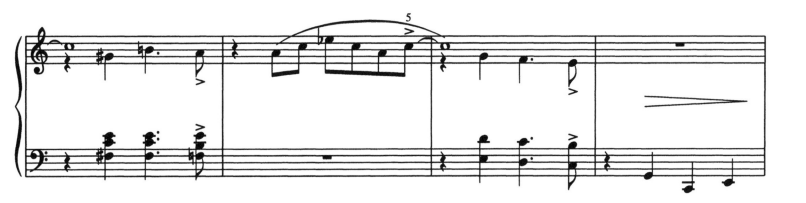

MY FOOLISH HEART

Words by NED WASHINGTON
Music by VICTOR YOUNG

Slowly with a beat

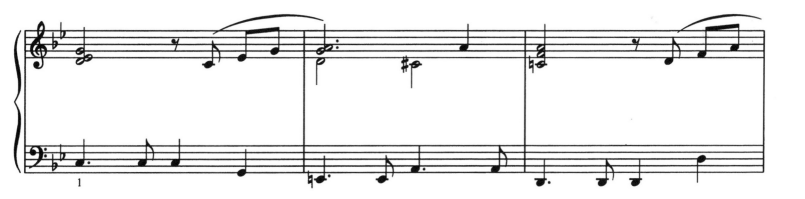

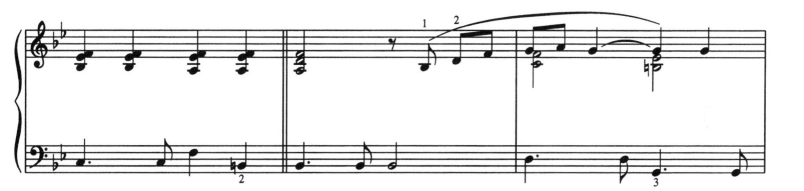

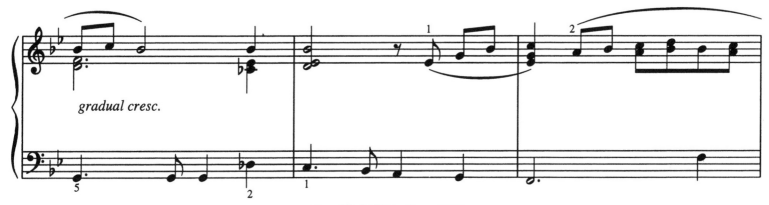

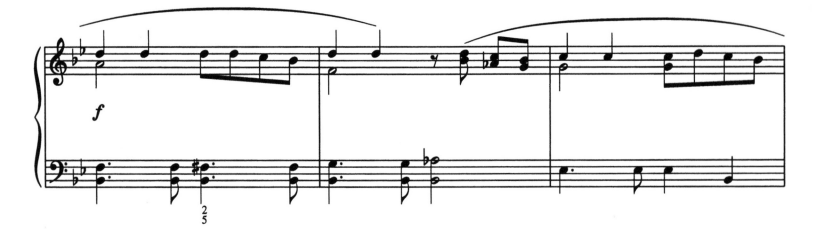

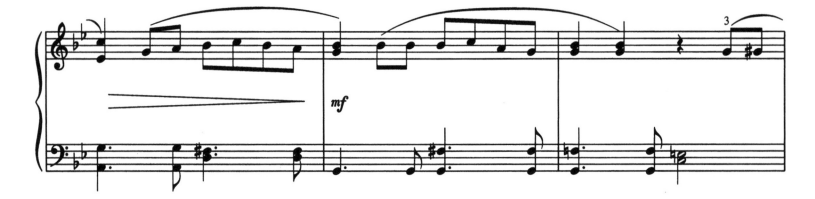

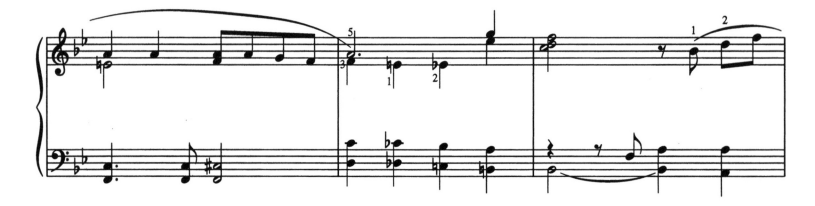

HAVE YOU MET MISS JONES?

(From "I'D RATHER BE RIGHT")

Words by LORENZ HART
Music by RICHARD RODGERS

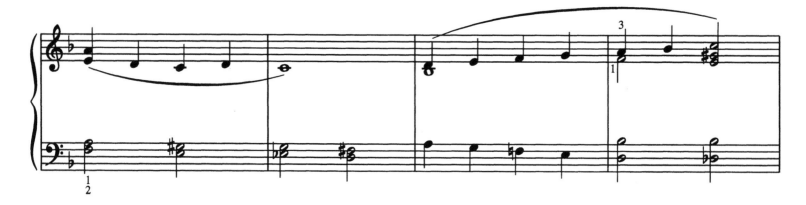

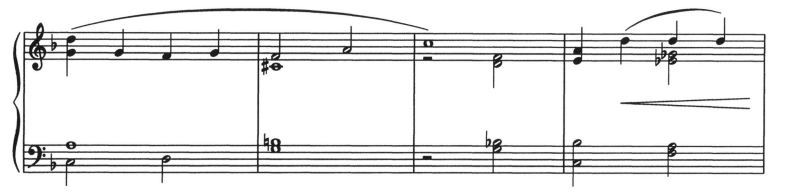

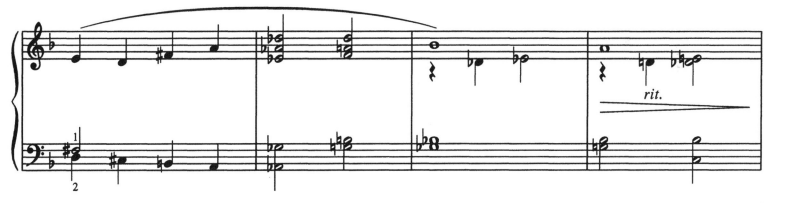

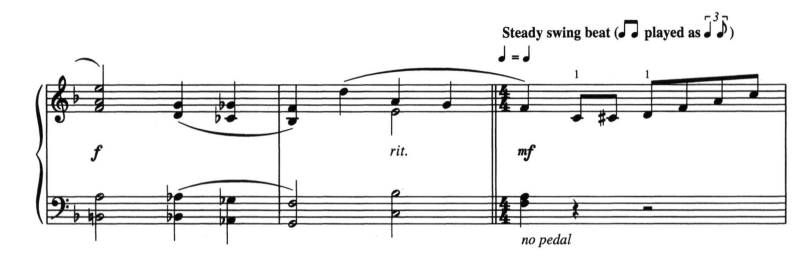

Steady swing beat (♫ played as ⅜♪)

♩ = ♩

f   *rit.*   *mf*

no pedal

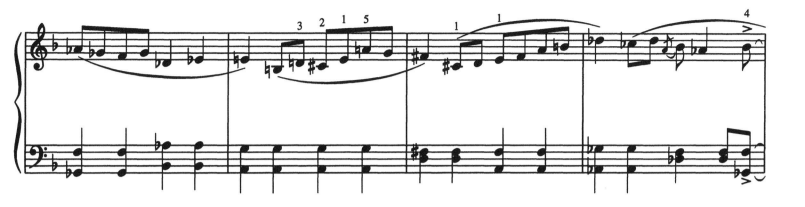

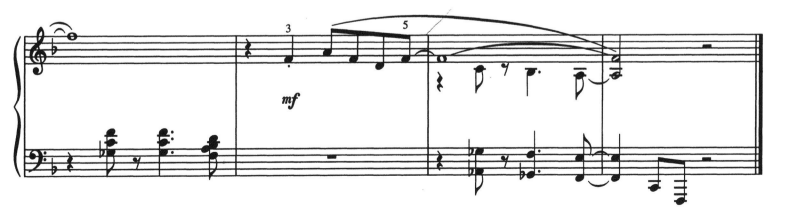

HOW HIGH THE MOON

(From "TWO FOR THE SHOW")

Words by NANCY HAMILTON
Music by MORGAN LEWIS

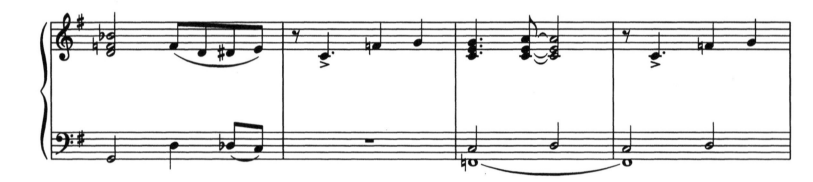

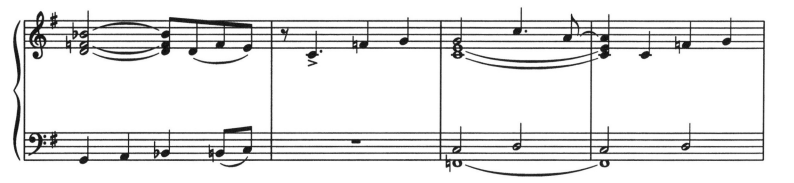

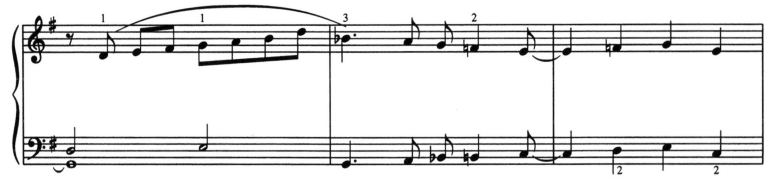

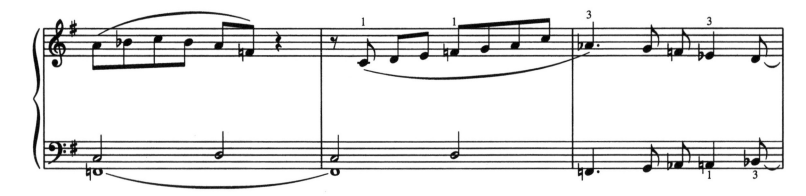

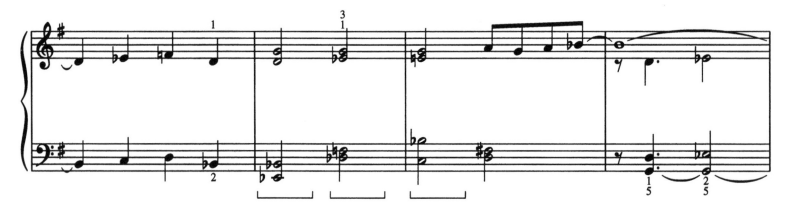

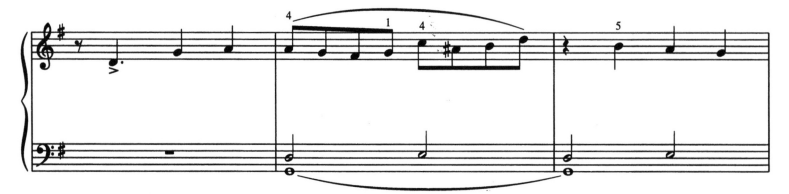

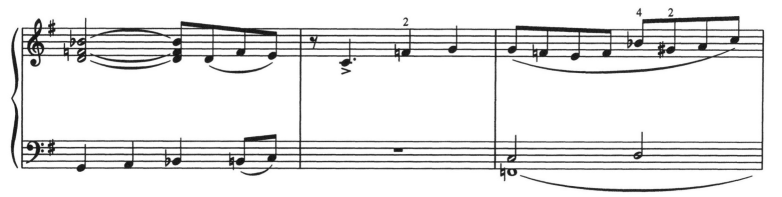

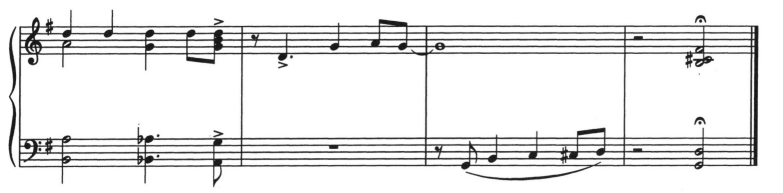

IN A SENTIMENTAL MOOD

Words and Music by DUKE ELLINGTON,
IRVING MILLS and MANNY KURTZ

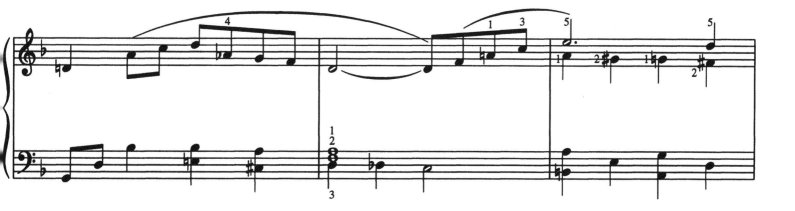

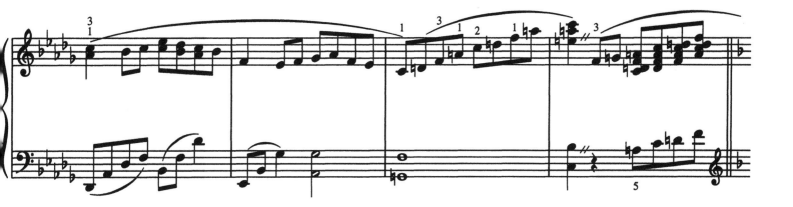

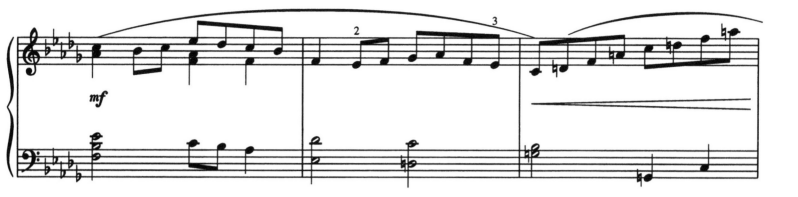

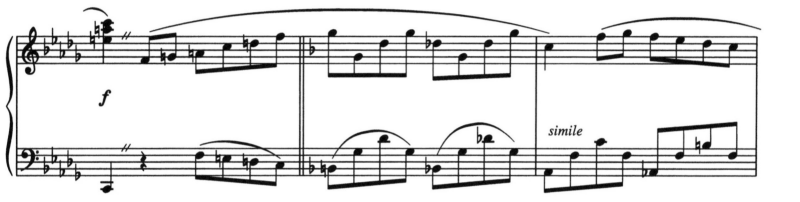

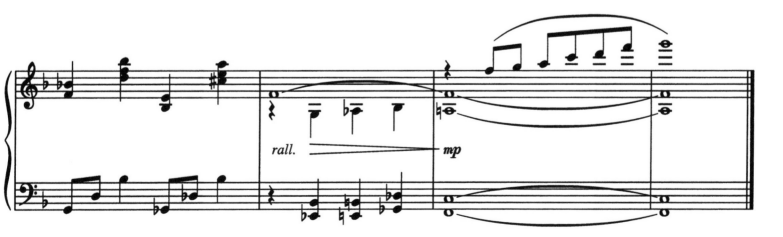

IT DON'T MEAN A THING
(If It Ain't Got That Swing)

Words and Music by DUKE ELLINGTON
and IRVING MILLS

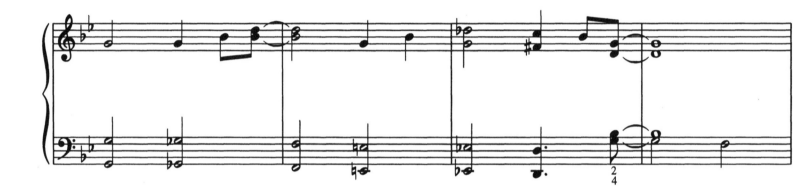

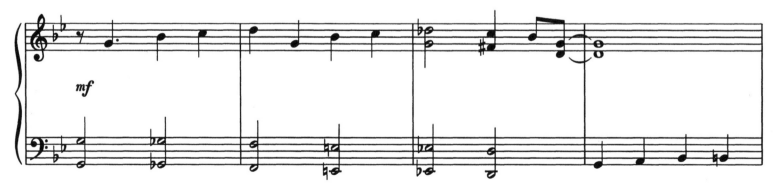

gradual cresc.

f

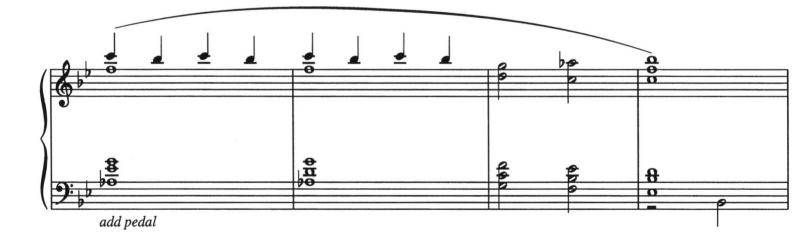

add pedal

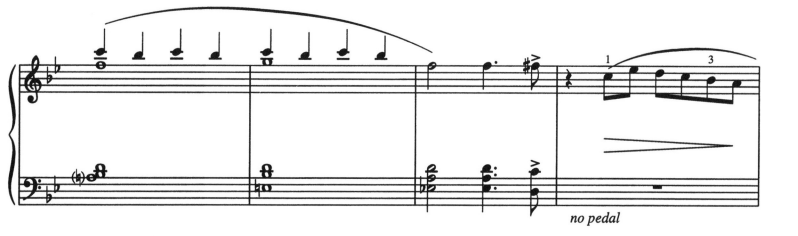

no pedal

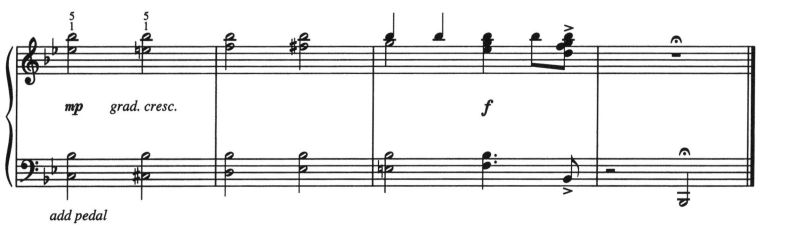

MY FAVORITE THINGS

(From "THE SOUND OF MUSIC")

Lyrics by OSCAR HAMMERSTEIN II
Music by RICHARD RODGERS

Moderately fast

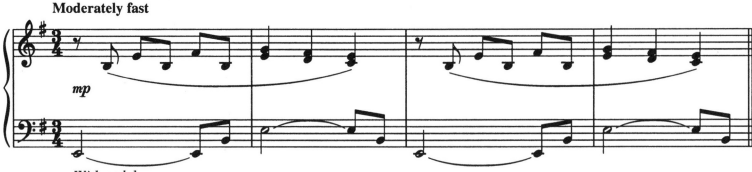

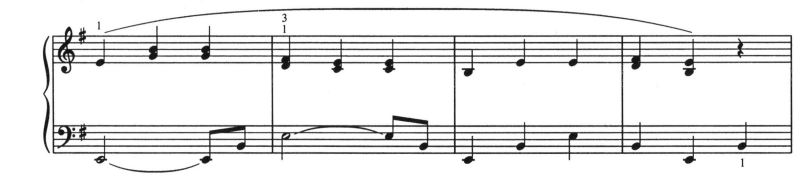

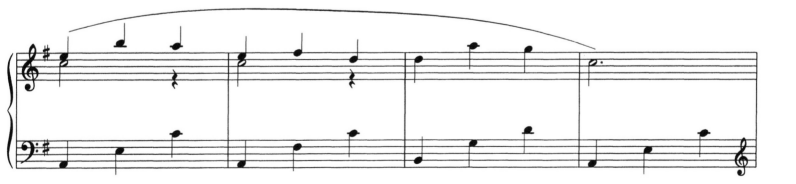

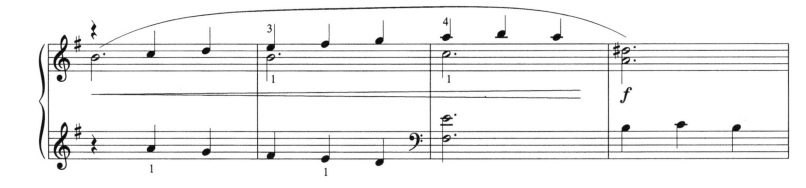

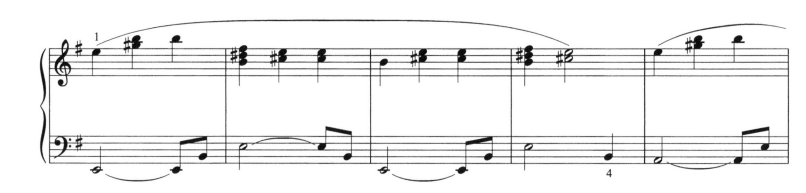

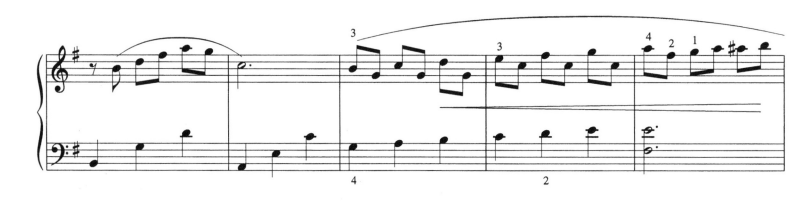

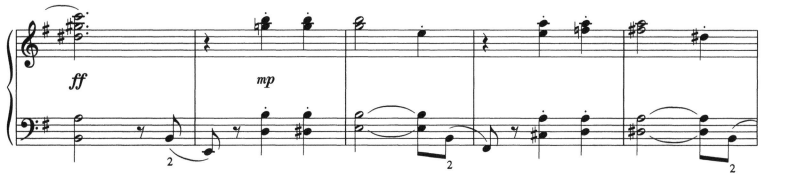

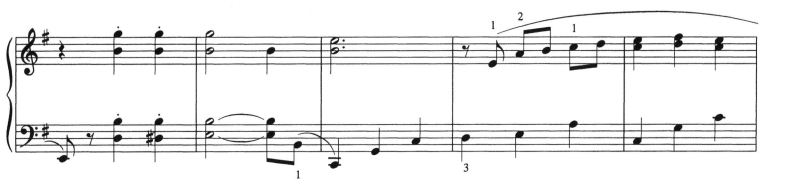

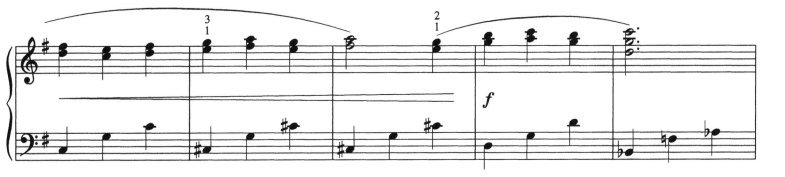

A NIGHT IN TUNISIA

Music by JOHN "DIZZY" GILLESPIE
and FRANK PAPARELLI

Moderately

MCA music publishing

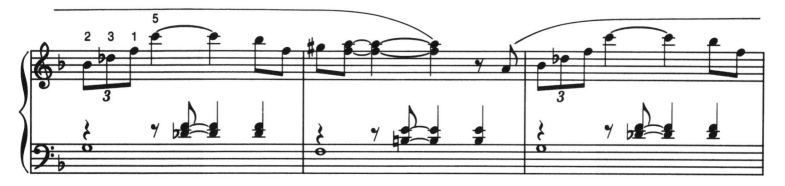

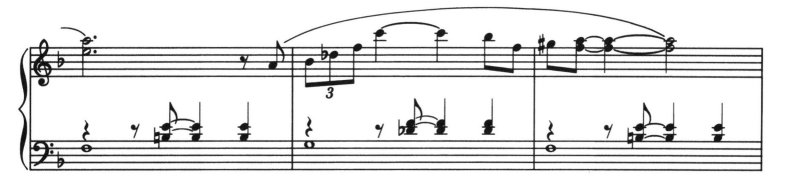

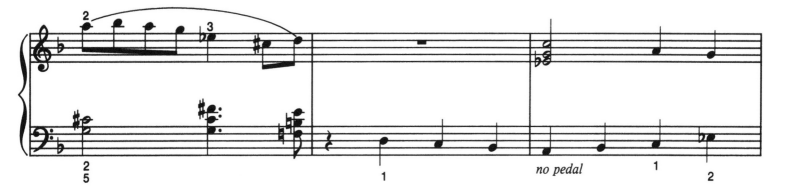

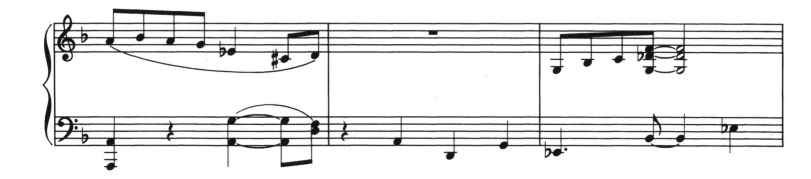

SOLITUDE

Words and Music by DUKE ELLINGTON,
EDDIE De LANGE and IRVING MILLS

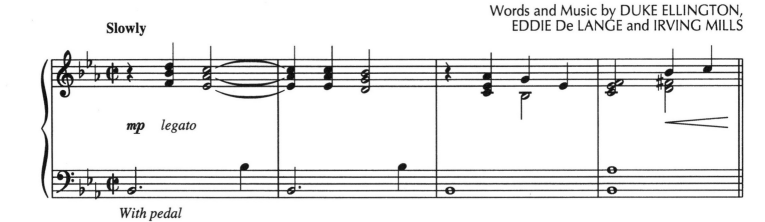

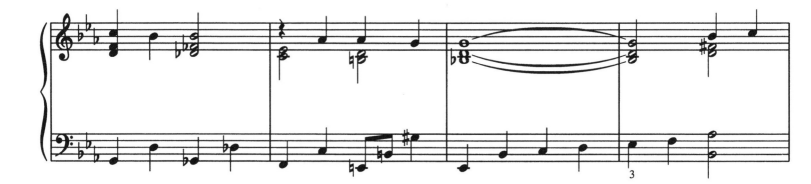

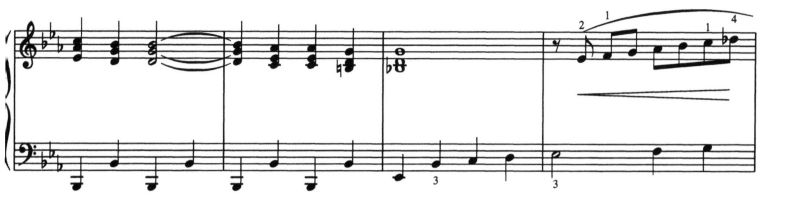

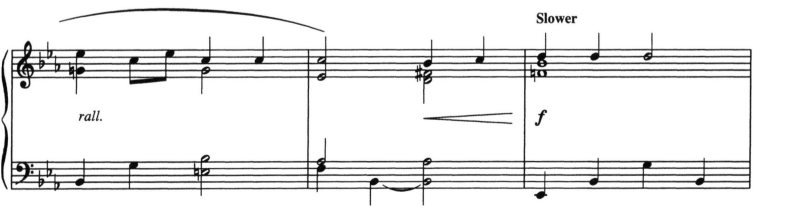

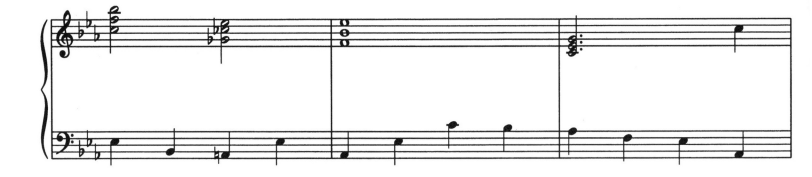

Slow with a beat (♩♪ played as ♪³♪)

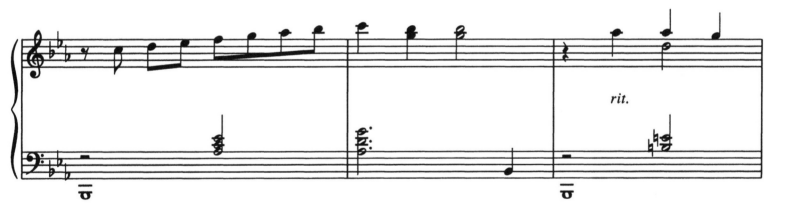

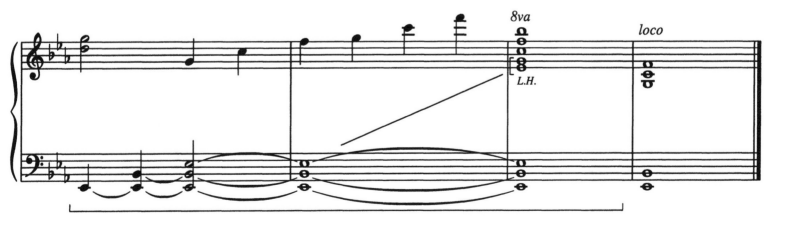

SOPHISTICATED LADY

Words and Music by DUKE ELLINGTON,
IRVING MILLS and MITCHELL PARISH

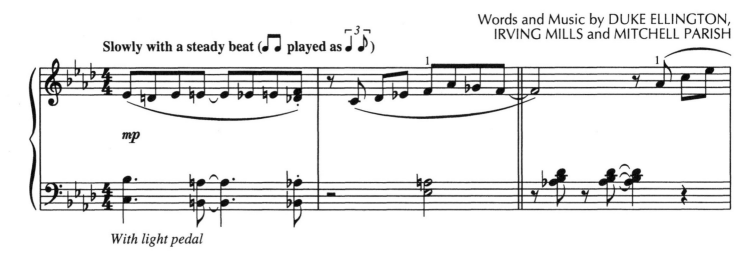

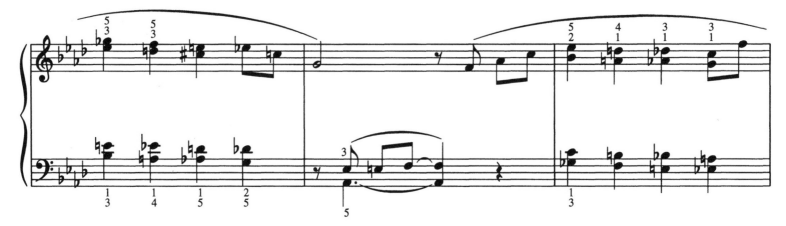

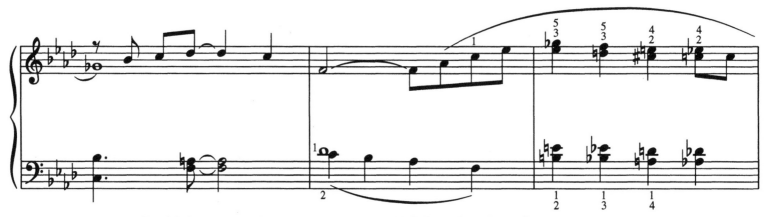

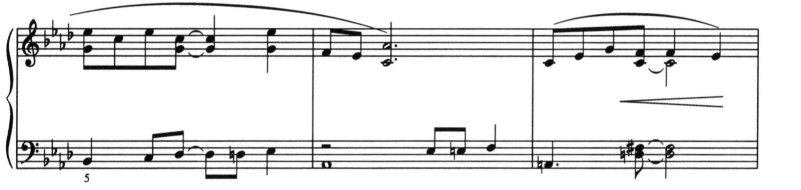

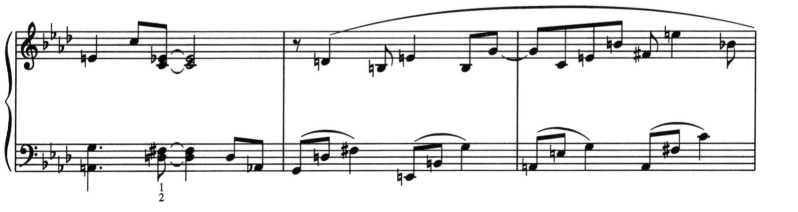

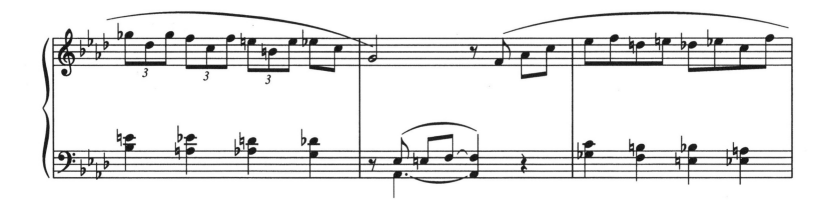

THE VERY THOUGHT OF YOU

Words and Music by
RAY NOBLE

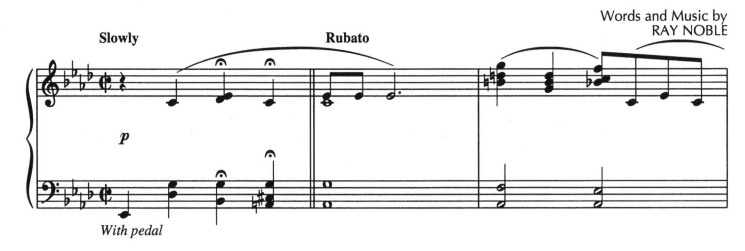

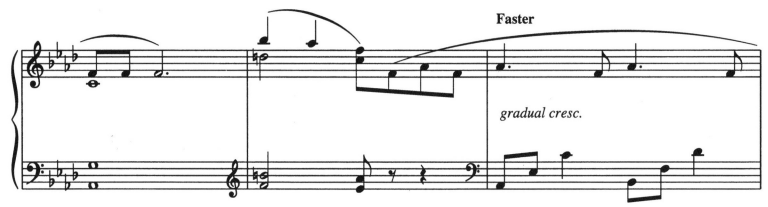

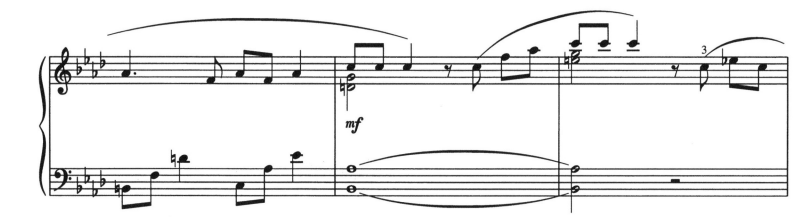

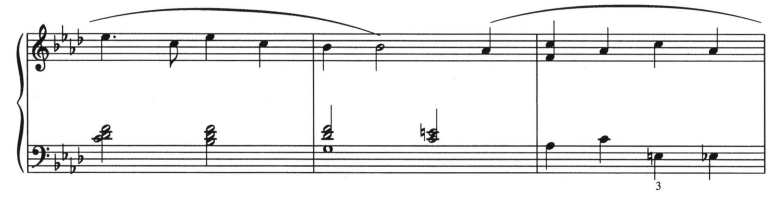

rit.　　　　　p　　　a tempo　　　　　rit.

Medium swing (♩♩ played as ♩♪³)

mf

light pedal

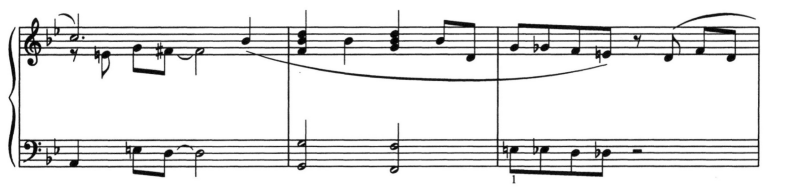
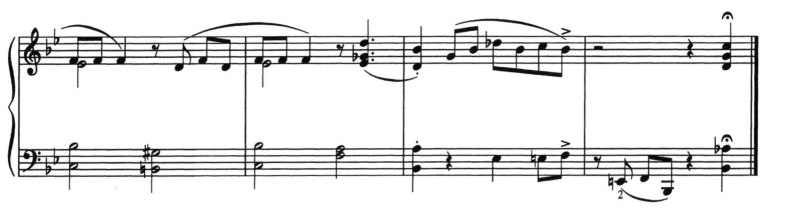

THE NEARNESS OF YOU

(From The Paramount Picture "ROMANCE IN THE DARK")

Words by NED WASHINGTON
Music by HOAGY CARMICHAEL

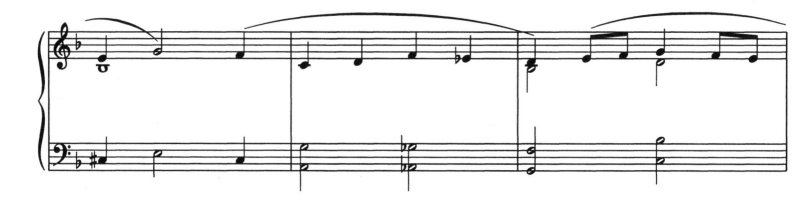

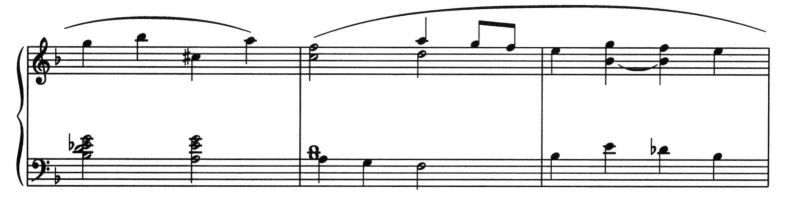

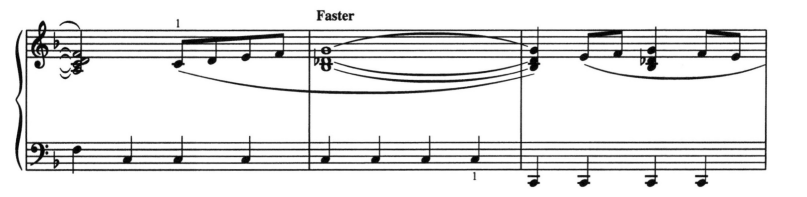

Faster

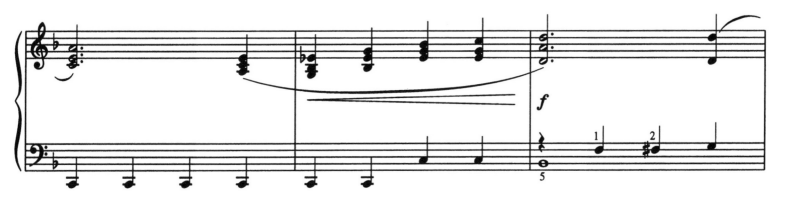

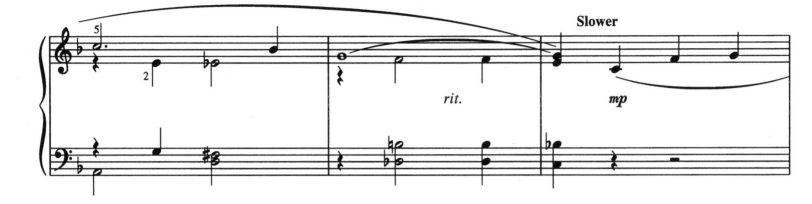

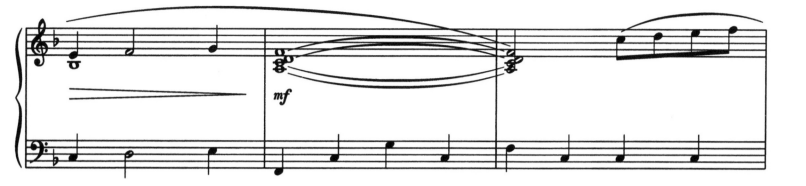

Steady tempo

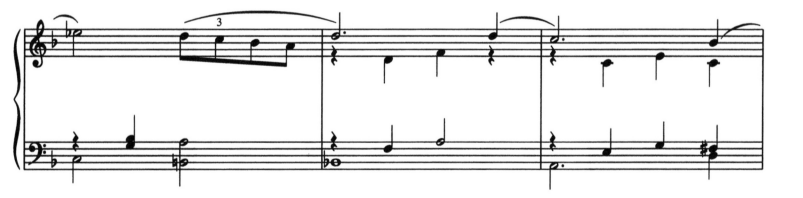

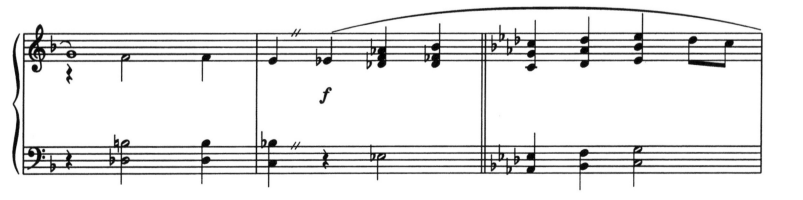

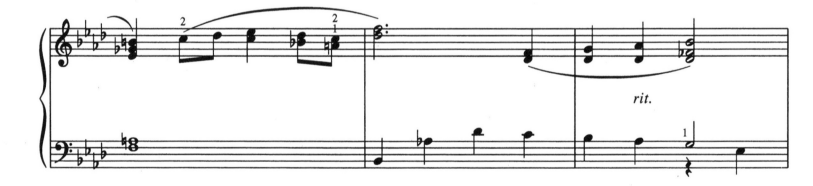

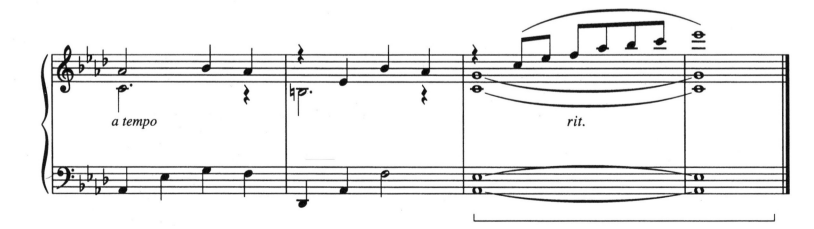